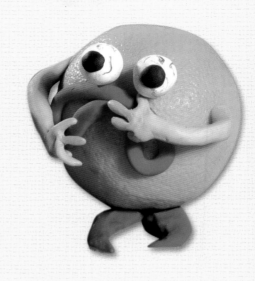

Published by the Penguin Group
Penguin Books Ltd, 80 Strand, London WC2R 0RL, England
Penguin Ireland, 25 St Stephen's Green, Dublin 2, Ireland
Penguin (Group) Australia, 250 Camberwell Road, Camberwell, Victoria 3124, Australia
Penguin Books India (P) Ltd, 11 Community Centre, Panchsheel Park, New Delhi 110 017, India
Penguin Group (NZ), cnr Airborne and Rosedale Roads, Albany, Auckland 1310, New Zealand
Penguin Books (South Africa) (Pty) Ltd, P O Box 9, Parklands 2121, South Africa

Penguin Books Ltd, Registered Offices: 80 Strand, London WC2R 0RL, England

© Brandmaster Limited 2006
Violent Veg ®
Website at: www.violentveg.com

First published by The Penguin Group 2006
Copyright © Penguin Books Ltd. 2006
Under licence from Brandmaster Limited 2006

ISBN-13: 978-1-84646-176-7
ISBN-10: 1-8464-6176-6

Printed in China

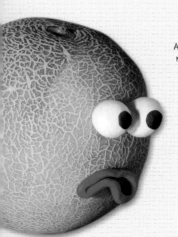
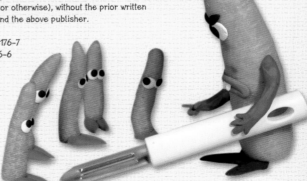

GALLERY 1

IS THIS THE REAL LIFE?
IS THIS JUST FANTASY?

FREDDIE MERCURY, QUEEN

It was back in late 2004 that word first reached us of the existence of an alien, albeit strangely recognisable culture. These living organisms chose not to plant this inkling into the consciousness of someone who might do something sensible with it (Stephen Hawking, for example, or the Gardener's Question Time panel). Instead, for an as yet unexplained reason, they selected a slightly long-in-the-tooth creative genius working on a trading estate just outside Birmingham.

We surmise this was because the said creative, who we shall call John, had been heard to complain about being forced occasionally to make a cup of tea for his colleagues despite possessing a brain the size of a planet. Notwithstanding his cerebral likeness to Uranus, John felt an irresistible urge to act upon this alien implantation, expounding its merits to his business colleagues Ian and Guy whilst claiming it as his creation. After all, who might contradict him in his own lifetime?

But let me rewind a little and explain how we got here in the first place (no, this is not going to be a brief history of thyme, but more an exposé of what brought about the confluence in the lives of three sages whose combined acumen has now given the world access to Violent Veg for all to enjoy).

John worked much of his life in and around the field of advertising and marketing, and has an entrepreneurial streak that saw him set up and run his own agencies. Ian gravitated from playing DJ around the nightclubs of Europe to become a successful sales director. Guy spent 12 years gazing at his naval career before swapping a life on the ocean wave for a life in mufti. In the mid-1990s, fate decreed that Ian would join forces with Guy in a marketing logistics business, and Ian sold their service to John's agency. John looked upon the service that was being delivered, and he was pleased. So John created another company and enticed Ian and Guy to build it with him, using the complementary business skills that they possessed. And thus was born a triumvirate which built up said business over 6 years before selling it in 2004 for a hill of beans; which was to be not the first time that vegetables interfered with John's brain.

The three amigos decided that, rather than spend the rest of their lives helping others to build their brands, they would create their own. And thus was born JIGAJIG. "What's that got to do with the price of spuds?" I hear you ask. Well, to cut a very long story short, they created a t-shirt (one of many, for JIGAJIG is primarily a t-shirt brand) with a silly image of a potato character having his head caved in with a hammer. People being what they are (sick and twisted) found this image highly amusing. This fact did not escape John's attention and sparked the concept of vegetables being violent to each other and Vegetarians being cruel and heartless. And lo, a whole new parallel universe was born (in less than 7 days too, I might add).

A few scribbled cartoons were presented nervously to his usually cynical colleagues. Guy and Ian didn't laugh the idea out, but did laugh at the idea: Violent Veg! Soon ideas and captions came flooding, test shots were done and the three were confident enough to take Violent Veg to the compost heap that was the Brand Licensing show in London, where it was received with great acclaim. From this germinated over the following year a successful range of greeting cards, posters, electronic games, etc as well as this wonderful, wonderful book.

We hope, dear Reader, you find that Violent Veg reflects a world which can make you laugh and can, if you peel an onion at the same time, make you cry too. It should be a balm to everyone who seeks the "holy grail" antidote to that horrible political-correctness we humans have allowed our leaders to foist upon us. So enjoy! And remember that in the world of the humble vegetable (and fruit), there's probably a potato who's about to sit back and embark on a similarly riotous book called "Horrible Humans".

John Knight: writing, modelling and art direction

Ian Shipley: photography, sets and lighting

Guy Barnard: writing, graphics and post-production

THE CRIMINAL UNDERWORLD

As with any highly developed society, there is a hierarchy in the world of Violent Veg within which all members have their place. Except the criminal fraternity. These guys inhabit the darker side, a terrifying underworld of naughtiness and spite. Meet the thuggish Alley Carrots who jealously guard their patch from unwelcome intruders. Dare to witness the murky secret of Eddie's country cousin. Identify, if you can, the root vegetable of all evil.

1808/78

AL "BEATER" CAROTENE, INFAMOUS FOR TORTURING HIS OWN BROTHER WITH A PEELER

When the prisoner found his cell door open,
he decided to make a bolt for it...

The melon was furious about
being wrongly picked out by the dyslexic victim...

There was no doubt about it,
they were now looking for a cereal killer...

Eddie's country cousin was a closet cannibal...

The carrots had a pea up against the wall...

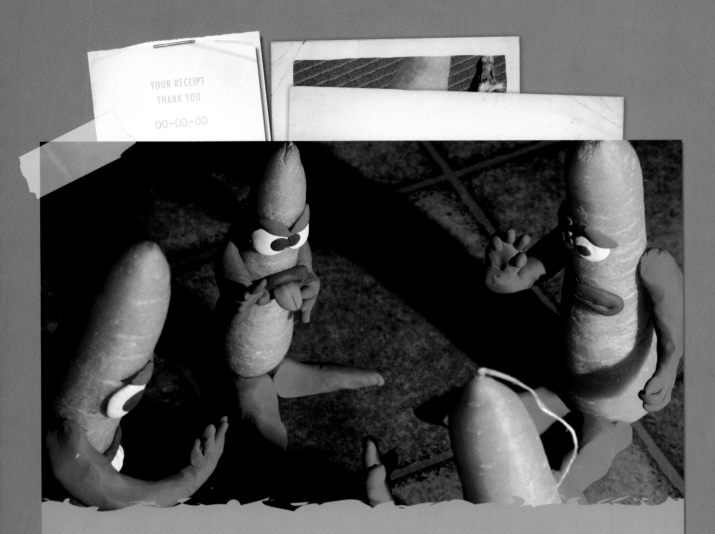

The argument got heated as the carrots debated
how many of them constituted a bunch...

Only when Barry got it home,
did he realise he'd bought a real lemon...

STRANGE NATURE

In the parallel universe of Violent Veg, things can sometimes seem a little strange, even weird. The behaviour and reactions of some fruit and veg are not necessarily as you'd expect, be it surreal role reversal or general predatory unpleasantness. And that's what makes them a most fascinating subject for anyone interested in parapsychobotanoeugenics.
Whatever that is.

After a liquid fertiliser lunch,
the pumpkin popped out for a leek...

The mange tout lived up to their
fearsome reputation...

The banana stripped off
and lay in wait for an unsuspecting monkey...

Breaking wind, even at sea, did not endear the helmsman to the first mate...

Tom swam for his life...

...but the currants were too strong for him

The coconuts suddenly heard the subliminal
drumming of hooves...

The homesteader very much regretted going round to complain about the Red Onions' war party...

FAMILY & RELAXATION

A vegetable's rack is his castle, especially where Mr Couch-Potato with his remote control is concerned. There's always a dull moment in the Couch-Potato household, as they endeavour sloth-like to live life to the min while keeping their backsides glued to the sofa, their eyes on the TV and their jaws round a burger.

Yet there are other families in the world of Violent Veg who have far less abnormal lives and for whom the day-to-day problems of life so closely reflect those of us humans; and that must really spook them sometimes.

When there was nothing on TV, the Couch-Potatoes
were fascinated by their own reflections...

Nothing uplifted the Couch-Potatoes' spirits like watching the omnibus edition of EastEnders...

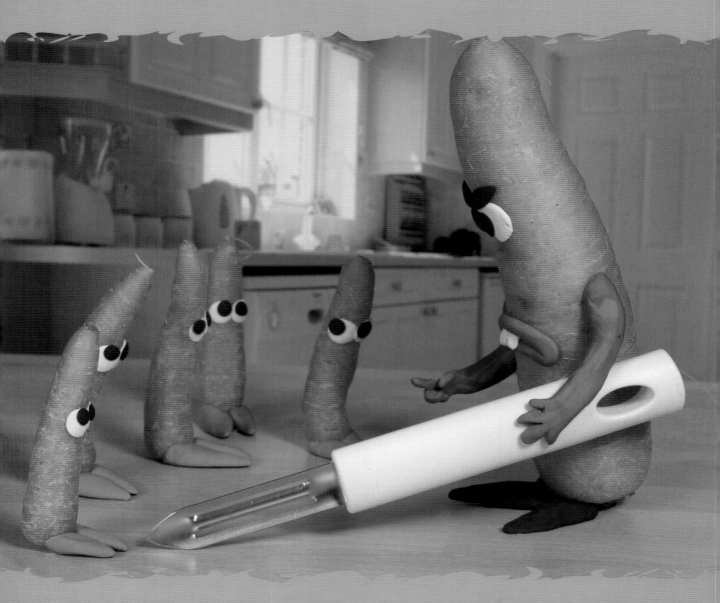

Mummy Carrot told the baby carrots that if she caught
them playing with the peeler again, she'd skin them alive...

They found that not only had they been separated at birth but, amazingly, both were called Arthur Cucumber...

Mr Couch-Potato re-asserted his authority over possession of the remote control...

Stung by criticisms of laziness,
the Couch-Potatoes took up their new hobby,
extreme channel-hopping...

To get some exercise, the kids agreed
to play football with Dad...

The baby sweetcorns tried to
butter up their mummy on Mother's Day...

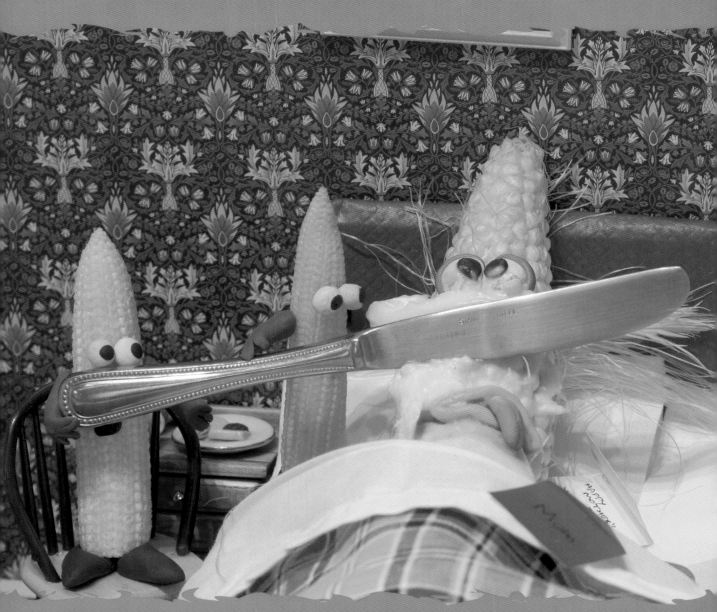

The Couch-Potatoes relaxed even more
than usual at Christmas...

LIFE IN ~~THE~~ HELL'S KITCHEN

Oh, the tragedy of every vegetable's life: the terrible realisation of a horrible death just so that evil Vegetarians can satisfy their craving for politically-correct calorie-deficient grub. So next time you sit down to eat your Sunday nut roast with all the trimmings, spare a thought for the defenceless vegetables that gave their lives for you and raise a glass and toast them. Or bake them or boil them or whatever.

The sage and onions were looking at a fate even worse than a fate worse than death...

It was easy to imagine how the whistling carrot grated...

The sweet potatoes were led to the chopping board,
like yams to the slaughter...

Mercifully, the smallest peas were able
to make good their escape...

Suddenly, the Vegetarian's fridge didn't seem quite such a bad place after all...

The carrots, the onion and the bayleaf
made a complete laughing stock of themselves...

And the sprouts had been so looking forward to a
nice day off this Christmas...

The sweet potato broke open one of the Vegetarian's fortune cookies and it didn't bode well...

OFFICE LIFE

Corporate life is not the tough number that busy executives would have us believe. Witness the Conference Pears, who spend their lives in fruitless meetings, dealing with non-core issues that give them the pip, forever pushing the envelope (but never wondering what's inside it), finding ways to avoid reaching decisions other than when the next meeting is going to be, and saving their most eloquent repartee for the bickering over the sandwich platter. So who does all the work, one wonders?

Not them, that's for sure.

Hazel handed in her notice, because she was
tired of working for peanuts...

The Conference Pears made many fruitless attempts to send and receive e-mails on their new Blackberries...

The boss walked into the meeting room and reiterated that <u>budgets</u> must be slashed...

The R&D Department demonstrated its prototype sex machine, which appeared to go down really well...

The meeting stared in disbelief as the agency outlined its creative strategy...

The last sandwich stand-off went on late into the night...

The best thing about Eddie's new job was
the huge celery...

Next Monday was looking tight in their diaries, and only one Conference Pear appeared to have a window...

The prickly pear insisted on getting his point across...

The Finance Director told his colleagues to focus on the bottom line...

The Conference Pears were issued with company rulers to help them improve their margins...

LOVE & SEX

Like the rest of us, vegetables need some lovin', and it's not just chillies which are hot. Whether it's true love or the deep-down-and-dirty kind, there's someone (and something) for everyone, and a little soft spot pulsates beneath even the hardest vegetable skin as they respond to the natural urge to plant their seed. Mind you, the only kind of eroticism in their world is when the fruit and veg start going bad...

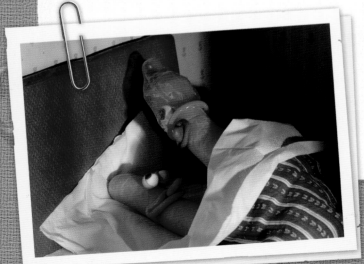

SENSIBLY, THE CARROTS PRACTISED SAFE SEX...

Mr Bramley's plums were in thrall
to Madamoiselle Dominatrix...

Mrs Bramley was most upset when she discovered her husband had been having an affair with the au pear...

The passion fruits pulled a cracker between them
at the Christmas party...

Mr Bramley gave the au pair a big goose for Christmas...

The agency hadn't properly explained that she would actually be meeting a Blind Date...

Mary didn't scrub up too badly for
an old potato...

Kevin had spent the entire day downloading corn off the internet...

The Blind Dates waited for hours,
not realising the other had also turned up early...

On first meeting, the pear found the passion fruit a little overbearing...

TRAVEL

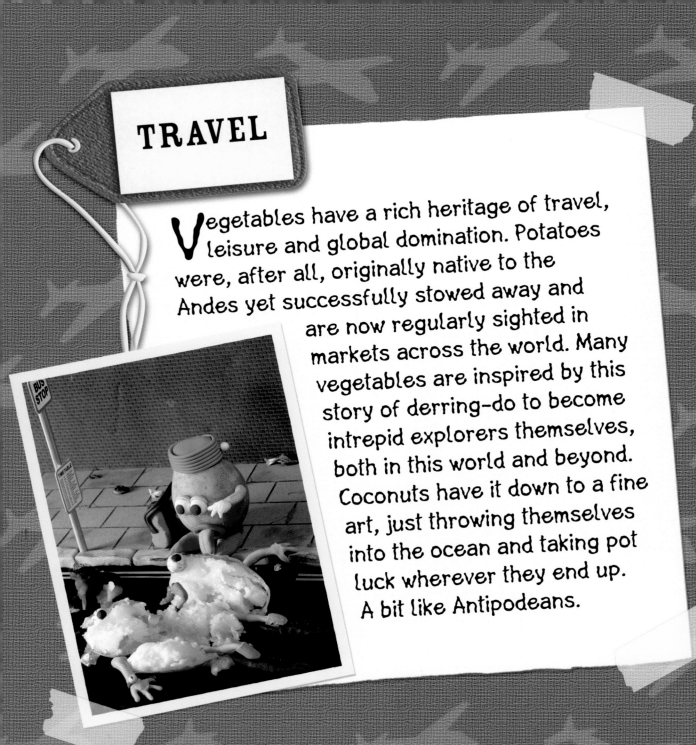

Vegetables have a rich heritage of travel, leisure and global domination. Potatoes were, after all, originally native to the Andes yet successfully stowed away and are now regularly sighted in markets across the world. Many vegetables are inspired by this story of derring-do to become intrepid explorers themselves, both in this world and beyond. Coconuts have it down to a fine art, just throwing themselves into the ocean and taking pot luck wherever they end up. A bit like Antipodeans.

Even King Cnut couldn't stem the tide of
EU Health & Safety legislation...

The aubergine was furious at being charged
for excess cabbage...

The peas suddenly realised the promised trip
to Iceland was a con...

Unfortunately, Monsieur and Madame Haricot-Verts
didn't speak English...

Mrs Bramley wondered if her husband would fancy Turkey again this Christmas...

The Cox's pilgrimage to New York was deemed a failure when they couldn't actually find the Big Apple...

The vegetables set out on a whaling expedition, simply to spite the Vegetarians...

The coconut asylum seekers came in search of paradise...

On arrival, the migrants were overwhelmed to be greeted
in person by the star-spangled banana...

U.S

LIFESTYLE

That great musician John Lemon, in a bitter twist, once said, "Life is what happens while you're busy making other plans." This final section is dedicated to those little moments that define us and our allotment in life. Except this time it's happening to vegetables. Enjoy!

Trudi tried to re-kindle her modelling career but sadly, in the intervening years, everything had gone a bit pear-shaped...

Eddie could have sworn he'd received the same present last year...

The oranges peeled off and did a complete pith-take of the full monty...

The Greens weren't really living up to their name
when they bought another 4 x 4...

Once he turned 50, Brian became strangely attracted to the colour beige...

Strangely, this was the third case of physalis
the doctor had seen this week...

The plumber was called when they found
a really bad leek in the bathroom...

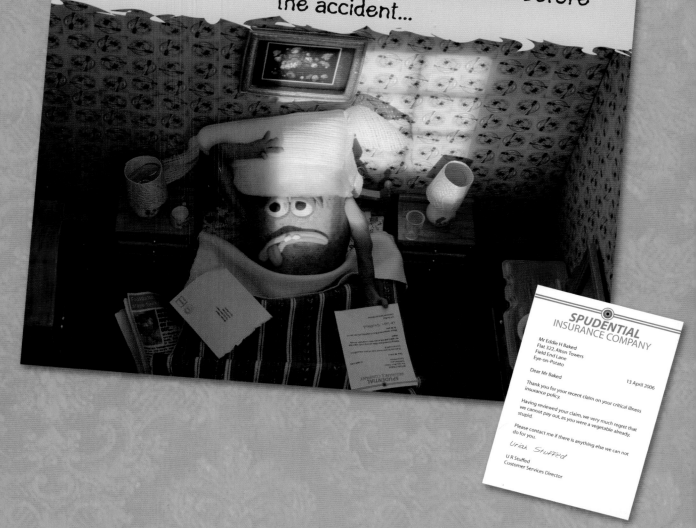

The apple was really cool with his new pPod...

The Blind Date and his faithful cauli became
inseparable companions...

EPILOGUE

We think you should know that we have received many strange stares as we rummaged through supermarket vegetable racks in search not just of the stars of the veg world but also of the ill-shaped and the unloved, in order to bring you this fascinating exposé.

On the plus side, however, we are indebted to our local greengrocer whose tolerance and understanding of the peculiar ways of three middle-aged (but indefatigably cheerful) men puts many a Care in the Community programme to shame.

And now the vegetables must bid you farewell for the time being: spending too long in the open is just asking for trouble from Vegetarians. If there is one message to take away when you close this book, it is that vegetables (and fruit) are living, sentient things, just like you. They feel, just like you. They hurt, just like you. And when you prick them, they seep juice. Almost like you.

So do yourself a favour: pop down to your local butcher and buy a lovely steak for dinner tonight instead. No chips, though.